Nature Journal

Notes on Nature Journaling

CLARE WALKER LESLIE

Yesterday I went for a walk with my nature journal. I live in a city. Granted, it is a green and leafy city, with plenty of front gardens and backyards. But still, it is a city, packed with cars and noise and people and sidewalks. I was about to teach an adult class called Drawing Nature in the Fall, and I needed to do some homework.

I took a side street from busy Massachusetts Avenue. This is the way I have walked our dog multitudes of times, for more than seven years. But this afternoon, because I had my journal and not the dog, I saw things quite differently. Try it and you'll agree. I was picking from the mush of the back street images of things I could draw that were "signs of fall." Before I knew it, I was drawing Indian pokeweed, smartweed, an ash seed, a foxtail grass, a partially eaten Bartlett pear fruit, a daddy longlegs.

I was sitting on the curb drawing stuff. People walked by. I was so absorbed, I barely noticed. I drew crabgrass, a black beetle, a maple seed, an acorn. I was totally hooked. I had not walked even fifty yards down the street and one hour had gone by. I heard the nearby buzzing sound of what I thought was an air conditioner. I followed the buzz. A mound of ivy on a fence was covered with hundreds of bees, madly plundering the flowers of pollen and nectar. I began drawing the bees: solitary bees, carpenter bees, sweat bees, flies; no yellow jackets, no butterflies.

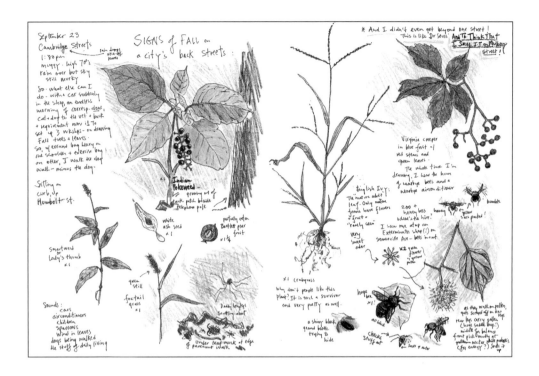

When I showed students my drawing, later on, they said, "How did you see all that?" I replied, "Because I've learned to pay attention." How do I describe the way we journal people feel about our pages? We clutch them to our chests and will not give them up, no matter what. Begin filling your journal with drawings and writings about daily nature observations and I guarantee you will discover an abundance of things to draw, a rise in general curiosity, and an intensified sense of connection with all around you. (Like me, you will find more people than you think love to bird watch, study butterflies, protect salamanders, and notice moon rises. They will genuinely admire your burgeoning journal.)

For some 30 years, I have been teaching people of all ages to see nature anywhere and to keep journals in whatever habitat and for whatever intention they choose. Journals are simply one of the most direct and personal ways of keeping in touch with the world around you, season by season, year by year. You can put whatever you want in your nature journal. But

I do suggest you always at least include the date, the place, the time, the weather, and the temperature to establish the nature journal's intent of studying ongoing events.

With environmental issues looming larger, we need to be the ones paying attention to what is out there, as well as what is not. The land cannot defend itself, nor can it speak. In the words attributed to the great Chief Seattle, "All things are connected like the blood that unites us. We did not weave the web of life, we are merely a strand in it. Whatever we do to the web, we do to ourselves."

How to begin your journal?

Begin by simply asking yourself questions like "What's happening outside at this time of year?" "What about nature makes me curious — birds, plants, insects, stars, rocks?" "What do I want to draw?" (You can ask yourself these questions while you're driving to work, cooking dinner, opening the mail, sitting in a boring meeting, or out for a walk.) Make a list in the margin of any page and transcribe it into your journal later: "sunny day, cat on a window ledge, cardinal singing, daffodils, apple blossoms out, wind in the trees, new moon." There you go. Take a walk with your journal, as I did on September 23, stopping for five minutes here and there to draw: a flower, an insect, a curious stone, an animal track, clouds, a bird flying by. Be sure to label each little drawing so it contains the information of your journal "stories."

DON'T be concerned with how well you draw. Label things or identify later from field guides available at the library or from your own growing library. I've written many books with the hope of helping nature journal people just like you. Learn about nature, however it suits *you* and wherever you are — in the city, the suburb, country, or by the ocean, or in the desert, mountains, or woods. Something is always happening outdoors. You can take three minutes to draw it, or three hours, or record it later from memory. (Don't worry if all you draw are stick figures. If you have never taken a drawing class, you are not expected to be able to draw well! If you have never taken juggling lessons, how are you expected to juggle well? Like any skill, drawing takes time, technique, practice, and patience. The more you use your journal, the better you will get.)

So have fun. Get going! Focus on what you are drawing and not on how well. Use pencil, colored pencils, ballpoint pen, watercolors — whatever you want to find your way. Often, in making a mistake, you find a new way. Cut things out and tape them into your journal, like articles on nature, drawings you have done in other places, or weather charts. Record your observations from day to day and month to month, creating your own seasonal record. Years later, I promise, you will come back to these pages and treasure them. I keep going back to mine, all the way to 1978 when I began.

Clare Walker Leslie

Neighborhood October 8

Turning Season in
Cambridge . MA
along Prentiss street + Frost street

2:30 pm - 4:15 pm
sunny, bright
but chilly
sunrise = 6:49 am
sunset = 6:14 pm
11 hrs 25 min light
darkness descending
— as the acorns
thud

Whole oak branches
of 6" length get
chewed off and
dropped — wham!

thwang!
whack!
Acorns hit cars,
fences, asphalt
as squirrels chase through
leaf mazes in arborways
above afternoon streets!
Familiar fall
sound of squirrel
"chirring" talk:
"mine"; "get away";
"eat this".

Some one sees me
standing with my
board, looking high
above and asks
"Tax assessor?"
I say "No, I'm drawing
a squirrel." He pauses and
then says "Well, well, in Cambridge
there is everything!"

Clare Walker Leslie
10·8·02

Suggested Equipment

The kind of equipment you use will vary according to where you are and what you want. I tend to keep my equipment as simple as possible so I am not weighed down and I don't have to worry about losing it or getting it wet. More careful studies can be done indoors when you have more time and want to make a really cool drawing.

Some people experiment with different colored papers, taping them into their journals as supplementary pages, or draw on other pages and then cut out and tape these into their journals. You can do a journal in many ways. But, an empty journal is — an empty journal.

Pens and Pencils

Some people have a favorite pen or pencil that makes their writing and drawing most enjoyable. Experiment until you find the instrument that has just the right weight in your hand, has the type of tip and thickness of line you like best, and moves along the paper surface smoothly. Pens and pencils respond differently to different kinds of paper and to different kinds of people. What works for me may not work for you the same way.

The fun of the journal is that you can experiment with styles and formats and mediums until you find what suits you best. It may even vary by season, time, or where you live.

Shoulder bag or back pack ready to go and not too complicated with lots of equipment —

Basics:

Hat, gloves, sunscreen, water bottle, folding stool (I rarely use) kept in bag

name tag

Nature Journal

A GUIDE TO BIRDS

INSECTS

binoculars are handy

eraser or eraser stick

Maybe a magnifying glass

black or blue ball point pen

Keep guides minimal: birds, wildflowers, insects at most. Have lots of guides at home.

HB or 2B technical drawing pencil

These are hundreds of disposable pens. Choose one that won't bleed through to the back side and holds a good line. I have used the "PILOT fineliner" for years. It "bleeds" when a wash is added but I like the effect. Permanent pens do not bleed.

I use technical drawing pens .25, .30, .50 but only at home. Some ink pens explode on airplanes!

Small knife to sharpen pencils and for clipping plants to draw.

Some metal sharpeners work. At home, I use a Panasonic battery run sharpener.

#6 or 8 brush – mid quality + price

25-30 basic colors of colored pencils and a case

I use a cheap box of watercolors in the field.

Small water bottle

clips or elastics to secure pages when windy

Decorate & make as simple or
as elaborate as you want

3. *Field Journal Page Setup*

Vary this format however suits you. I use my nature journal to study
nature as well as to draw it. I sequence through the pages of my journal,
going in order by the months. I make from 3–10 entries a month, but I am
a professional. You may make 1–50. Follow your time, your passion, your
subjects, your ecosystem.

❧ Top left or right of your paper :

*Can be recorded
before going outdoors*

**Find from newspaper, internet,
TV, or Farmer's Almanac*

- Date
- Place
- Weather/Temperature*
- Time of day
- Moon phase*
- Sunrise* ⎫
- Sunset* ⎭ *day length*
- Other observations like: Fall equinox,
  Hallowe'en, snow all day, drought

❧ Quietly outdoors, wander a bit to absorb the location.
  - RECORD personal responses & sounds: hot, buggy, sleepy;
  hear: leaves rustling, blue jay, crow.
  - DRAW in 3–5 minutes each: 2 ground plants, 2 leaves, 2 flowers,
  1 insect, 2 fruits, 1 bird, 2 trees (3"x 5").

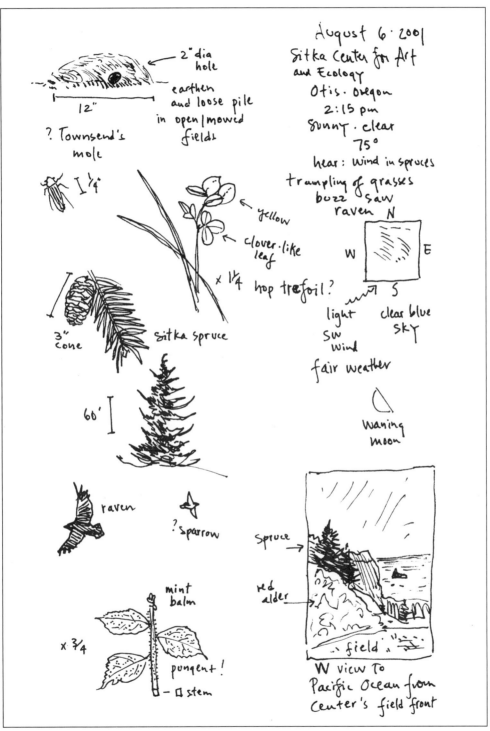

2" dia hole

12"

earthen and loose pile in open/mowed fields

? Townsend's mole

I 1/4°

× 1 1/4

3" cone

Sitka spruce

60' I

yellow

clover-like leaf

hop trefoil?

raven

? sparrow

mint balm

× 3/4

pungent!
— □ stem

August 6 · 2001
Sitka Center for Art
and Ecology
Otis · Oregon
2:15 pm
sunny · clear
75°
hear: wind in spruces
trampling of grasses
buzz saw
raven

N

W   E

S

light
SW
wind

clear blue sky

fair weather

waning moon

spruce →

red alder

field

W view to
Pacific Ocean from
Center's field front

Sample format for field journal page.

Exercise 1. **Blind Contour**
• Look only at object, never at your drawing.
• Start in one place and, with a continuous line, go over whole form — including inside veins, lines, marks.
• Don't lift your pen/pencil until finished.
• This will get the "sense" of the form in your hand.

Exercise 2. **Modified Contour**
• The same instructions as above, only now you can look at your paper, as well as at the object.
• Still don't lift your pen/pencil off the page.

I minute long!

These two exercises are *very* useful for getting to know an object and for helping you with Foreshortening.

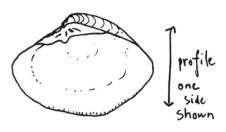

profile one side shown

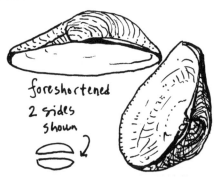

foreshortened 2 sides shown

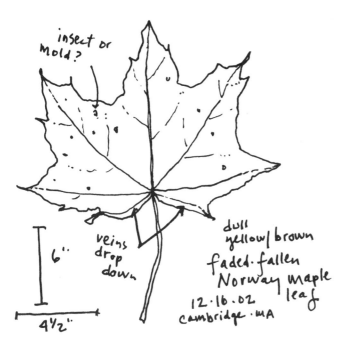

insect or
mold?

6"

4½"

veins
drop
down

dull
yellow/brown
faded · fallen
Norway maple
leaf
12·16·02
cambridge · MA

Exercise 3.

Field Identification Drawing

Often used in nature journal drawing — in pen or pencil with colored pencil or watercolor added.

For more tips on drawing specific aspects of nature and guidance in field observation, see the shaded pages at back of book.

I was hiking in the Pacific Northwest when I saw this bird. Not familiar with Western birds, I quickly drew it in the little journal in my pack. Later, I found a Western Guide and redrew it from its picture. Drawing helps you learn to identify birds.

V black

brilliant
orange

bright
yellow

sitting on branch
over fast flowing
creek
6·30
Mt Rainier Park · WA
3:30 pm

Western
♂ Tanager
breeding plumage

USING COLOR

Primary colors can be mixed to make the secondary colors:

RED + YELLOW = ORANGE

YELLOW + BLUE = GREEN

BLUE + RED = PURPLE

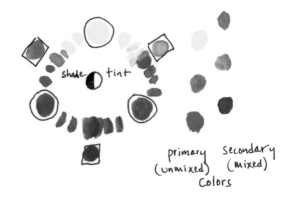

shade · tint

primary
(unmixed) · secondary
(mixed)
Colors

erasing

cream

white

Colored pencils do not mix colors like watercolor. They blend them.

A colored pencil drawing can take from 10 minutes to 10 hours.

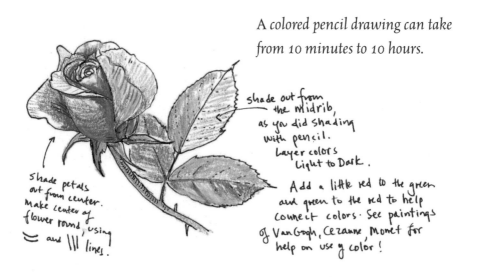

shade out from
the midrib,
as you did shading
with pencil.
Layer colors
light to Dark.

Add a little red to the green
and green to the red to help
connect colors. See paintings
of Van Gogh, Cezanne, Monet for
help on use of color!

Shade petals
out from center.
Make center of
flower round, using
≅ and \\\ lines.

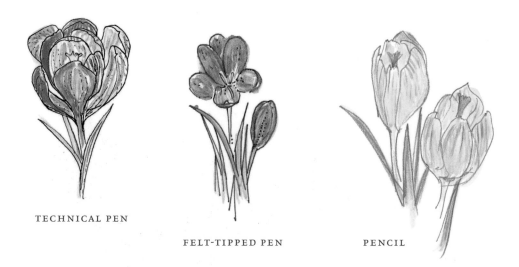

TECHNICAL PEN

FELT-TIPPED PEN

PENCIL

COLORED PENCILS are used a
great deal in the field for quick
color notations, as done here:

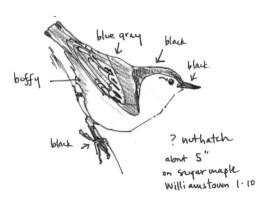

blue gray

black

black

buffy

black

? nuthatch
about 5"
on sugar maple
Williamstown 1·10

Let pencil lines
show if you want

mop out
extra color
with
paper towel

try pen
and
watercolor

wet
on
wet

dry on
wet

let colors
puddle

Try using a wash of
water on a brush over
a PEN-AND-INK
drawing.

WATERCOLOR
& PENCIL

TECHNICAL PEN
& WATERCOLOR

(Drawn in the car and
colored from memory later.)

11·17·95
3pm
darkening
late fall

Rte 12 N
The road to
Keene NH

PENCIL & COLORED PENCIL

(Drawn in the car watching coyote.)

Nov. 28
Out on Duxbury Beach
@ 3 - Sun low
A "see nothing" day.
when - tawny buff
marsh grasses becomes
a coyote!
Anna noticed the
yellow eyes.
Did he/she have
Something under a
paw?

watches us —

A new journal begun—
How brave to march off
onto blank pages—
One foot lifted in the air
wondering where
it will land . . .

Don't worry if you can't think of what to draw or where to begin. Just begin. There are things to discover everywhere, at any time. Above all, have fun. As one inner-city teacher commented, "Nature? At least we can draw the sky."

The journal was my only companion.
I took it everywhere on my long walks
into the open land, and we saw
the mysteries of the earth together . . .

— BURGHILD NINA HOLZER
A Walk Between Heaven and Earth

I am merely a watcher.
This is my observatory.

Put on your calendar an afternoon or morning when you can give yourself a long, focused time to use your journal. Perhaps take a weekend trip or join a naturalists' group trip. If you can't find that much time, taking even 15 minutes to draw a daylily blooming is plenty.

The study of nature is a limitless
field, the most fascinating
adventure in the world.

— MARGARET MORSE NICE
Research Is a Passion With Me

For those gloomy days when you can't be outdoors,
brighten your spirits by buying a bouquet of flowers.
Draw them and write about them. What do the
colors, shapes, and smells make you think about?
You might write just a sentence or two, a few
phrases, or even a poem.

Drawing takes total concentration.
You cannot think of any thing
other than what you are looking at.
You become It. It becomes You.

The speech of insects
and the speech of men
are heard with
different ears.

— SHIKI
17th century Zen poet

There is no one way to draw in a journal. Draw fast, slow, squiggly, sketchy. Add color and texture. Stand, sit. Use your opposite hand. Don't look at your paper. Have fun!

A nature journal is your own
personal HISTORY —
your own stories that will
go down in time.

Observe and record rain, snow, sleet, fog, wind storms, clouds, the sun and moon. Just think, one thing the dinosaurs saw that we still see today is — the sky.

....

....

....

....

....

....

....

....

....

....

....

*Drawing even the little things
helps to focus the mind,
calm the spirit. There's always
something to be drawn.*

There is a great deal of talk these days
about saving the environment.
We must, for the environment sustains
our bodies. But as humans we also
require support for our spirits, and this
is what certain kinds of places provide.
— ALAN GUSSOW, A Sense of Place

Add clippings from newspapers, magazines, note cards, or letters from friends to your journal when they relate to natural events.

You must walk sometimes
perfectly free, not prying nor
inquisitive, not bent on seeing things.
Throw away a whole day for a
single expansion, a single inspiration
of air . . . Nature will bear the
closest inspection. She invites us
to lay our eye level with
her smallest leaf, and take
an insect view of its plain.
— HENRY DAVID THOREAU

*What I
haven't drawn,
I don't
really know.*

....

....

....

....

....

....

....

....

....

....

....

*A watchful eye, a little extra
attention to detail, and
a sharpened sensitivity to
seasonal changes can uncover
a veritable Serengeti Park just
beyond the bedroom window.
All you have to do
is learn to see.*

— JOHN MITCHELL
A Field Guide to Your
Own Backyard

Sometimes on a walk, I will collect seeds,
leaves, shells, fruits, or small feathers and
bring them home to set on my desk. They
sit there until I draw them — maybe drawing
one at a time if I have only 10 minutes here,
15 minutes there.

MEMORY DRAWINGS

You won't always have your journal with you
when you see a cool event. Memorize basic
form, color, size, story, time, and place and
add to your journal when you get home.

The everyday places desperately need our attention —
partly because they are changing so fast, and not always
for the better, and also because tremendous benefit
is to be gained from a personal involvement
with your own locality.
— THE PARISH MAPS PROJECT, London 1987

Create a mini journal project. I spent one
August focused on drawing (or trying to draw)
the insects in our meadow as well as the insects
coming to our lights at night. Insects are
incredibly beautiful to draw and so varied.

The greatest gift the journal can give you is the TIME
to roam without purpose, to LISTEN, to WATCH,
to REFLECT, to be QUIET. How little quiet we have
in our lives.

I go to nature to rest
my eyes. I go to nature
to connect with something
broader than I can
understand.

Use your journal as an excuse to roam.
People smile and leave me alone when
they find me standing on the street,
staring at a fence. The presence of my
journal and pencil tells them I'm
drawing and am not in need of help!

Seeing and drawing can become one,
can become SEEING/DRAWING ...
No longer do I "look" at a leaf, but
enter into direct contact with its life.

— FREDERICK FRANCK
The Zen of Seeing

Bird feeders, local duck ponds,
nearby rivers, ocean coasts, and
sand beaches are all good places
to draw birds.

I take solace from nature
over and over when
I cannot understand
the human spirit.

The more you sketch . . .

the easier it is to draw . . .

— CYNTHIE FISHER
Wildlife Painting Basics

Not all journal pages need be images.
Sometimes I write a "shopping list"
of seasonal events as well as a list of
personal events in my own life.

I am a storyteller with my drawings.

Consider your nature study drawings as 5- to 10-minute field guide illustrations. You can't take the specimen with you, so carefully draw primary features, preferably in profile. Write descriptive details: color, texture, size, location, time, and date.

[Prince] Charles believes that the shape of a landscape,
whether urban or rural, has a profound effect
on the human spirit, influencing mental health,
personal behavior and economic activity.

— ROBERT BATEMAN
Thinking Like a Mountain

*I take notes
on Life.
I don't conclude
it or put it
in a frame —
It just lies here,
not judged —
in my journals.*

Treat the Earth well.
It was not given to you
by your parents.
It was lent to you
by your children.

— AFRICAN PROVERB

TREE PROJECT

Make an inventory of the trees that grow
in your area. Write descriptions of each;
measure the leaves, fruit, and buds; draw
a map indicating where each type of tree
is located; draw full tree silhouettes and
details of the twigs, buds, seeds, and dried
leaves as best you can.

I praise each day splintered down,
And wrapped in time like a husk,
A husk of many colors spreading,
At dawn fast over the mountains split.

— ANNIE DILLARD

You may not always like your drawings.
Yikes, they're in a bound book! Leave your
disasters in. You may later find you can,
or you did, improve on them. Only rarely
do I rip out some unbearable mess.

Follow your garden through the
year. Garden journals can be part of
your nature journal — the cultivated
garden and the wild garden beyond
your lawn mower.

Take a Microscopic View

If it is too cold or rainy for prolonged observation outdoors, take a walk and collect small specimens of twigs, dried weeds, galls, and the like. Then bring them indoors for a close-up study using your eyes and a magnifying glass. Record your observations in sketches and words.

In the pages of a journal . . . we can get better
at reading the body language of the world.
The overall expression of a season,
the vibrancy in a landscape, a garden, a cat,
the psychic atmosphere of a city street.

— HANNAH HINCHMAN
A Trail Through Leaves

LISTEN TO THE INSECT ORCHESTRA
On slow summer days, just sit outdoors and
listen to the insect orchestra. Try to observe
the individual players so you can match the
sound to the player. Look for edges of wings
being rapidly vibrated back and forth, or
legs rubbing on wings.

Narcissi, amaryllises, crocuses, irises, and tulips
are all spring flowers, but you can get a jump on
spring by growing them indoors. Start bulbs on a
windowsill, then record the daily changes as the
plants sprout, capturing the flowering activity
little by little until the plants reaches full bloom.

I use my journal to
connect with nature,
as it gives me space from
connecting with people.

When you can't find anything to draw,
there are always cloud patterns, moon
phases, leaves at your feet, insects
beside your path, squirrels in the trees,
or the path of the sun.

Sometimes it helps you get acquainted with local animals, birds, insects, and fish if you first draw them from good photos or the drawings in identification guidebooks. By drawing from the "still" animal you can draw the "moving" animal more easily.

We live as guests in the divinity of nature.

— CELTIC SPIRITUALITY
quoted by JOHN O'DONOHUE
in The Invisible World

Many of our observances have roots in the cycles of nature and the earth honored by ancient cultures. Record how differently people observe holidays and what elements from nature play a symbolic role in the celebration. For example, the Celts of early Europe celebrated the four great agricultural festivals of spring (February 1), summer (May 1), fall (August 1), and winter (November 1).

Make your own travel postcards. Draw little journal images of what you see onto postcards to send to friends, instead of photos.

LEAVES, TWIGS, AND BUDS

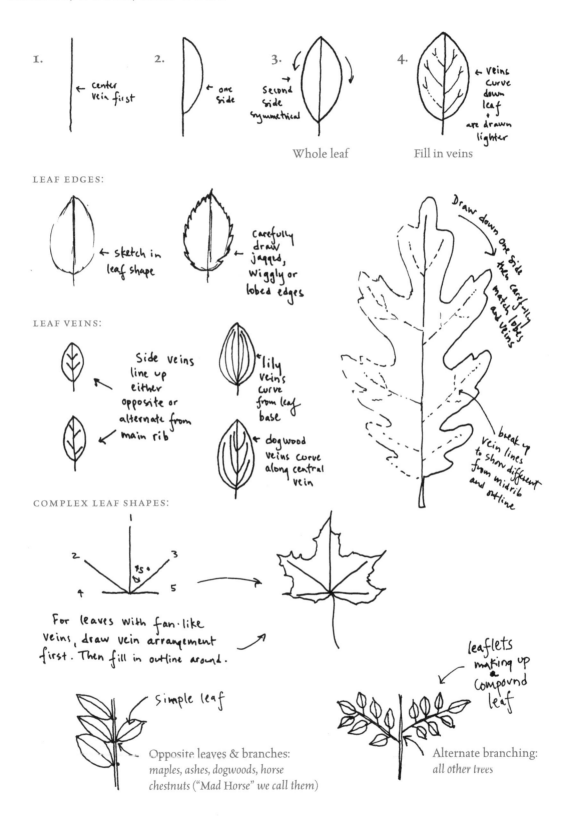

1. ← center vein first

2. ← one side

3. → Second side symmetrical

Whole leaf

4. ← veins curve down leaf & are drawn lighter

Fill in veins

LEAF EDGES:

← sketch in leaf shape

carefully draw jagged, wiggly or lobed edges

Draw down one side then carefully match lobes and veins

break up vein lines to show different from midrib and outline

LEAF VEINS:

Side veins line up either opposite or alternate from main rib

lily veins curve from leaf base

dogwood veins curve along central vein

COMPLEX LEAF SHAPES:

For leaves with fan·like veins, draw vein arrangement first. Then fill in outline around.

→ Simple leaf

Opposite leaves & branches: maples, ashes, dogwoods, horse chestnuts ("Mad Horse" we call them)

leaflets making up a compound leaf

Alternate branching: all other trees

shows foreshortening

shade out from veins

ORNAMENTAL CHERRY

PACHYSANDRA

draw where leaves change planes

① ② ③
shapes show foreshortening

WHITE OAK

Squirrel chewed acorns

Fruits, winter buds, and seeds are great to observe and draw:

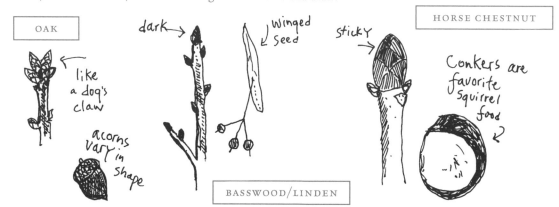

OAK

dark →

↓ Winged seed

sticky →

HORSE CHESTNUT

like a dog's claw

acorns vary in shape

Conkers are favorite squirrel food

BASSWOOD/LINDEN

DECIDUOUS TREES : SUMMER

1. Trees have different shapes. Observe overall shape first.

Deciduous trees have leaves that fall off each autumn, to save water loss in winter and to prevent extra weight in ice or snow storms.

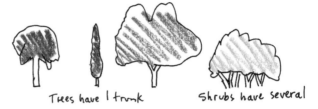

Trees have 1 trunk

Shrubs have several

2.

A contour drawing can help you see the shape

3. Now draw the trunk up from the base to where leaves begin

4. Make marks on your paper and draw the tree within those marks, no more than 6" or 7". A full page takes too long.

5.

SUGAR MAPLE

oak

← leaf shapes symbolized →

maple

dogwood birch alder

sumac hickory

5a. Shade out in a ring — to get a sense of roundness on a flat piece of paper

5b. Draw major leaf masses as they catch light and dark shadows. Draw in branches as they appear betwen leaf masses. Put in shadows on the trunk, if you want.

6. Draw parts of the tree:
- buds & twigs
- seeds & fruits
- leaves
- any evidence of animal activity

← leaf nest in tree is made by squirrels

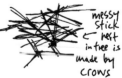

messy stick nest in tree is made by crows

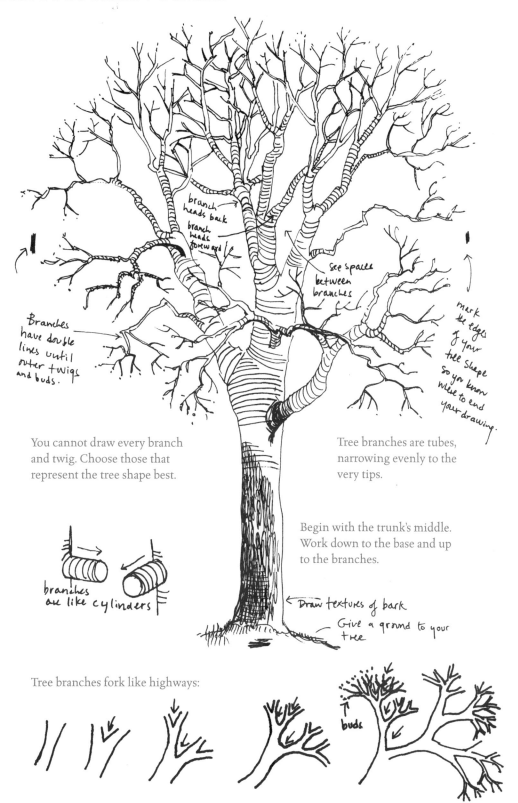

branch
heads back

branch
heads
forward

see spaces
between
branches

mark
the edges
of your
tree shape
so you know
where to end
your drawing.

Branches
have double
lines until
outer twigs
and buds.

You cannot draw every branch
and twig. Choose those that
represent the tree shape best.

Tree branches are tubes,
narrowing evenly to the
very tips.

branches
are like cylinders

Begin with the trunk's middle.
Work down to the base and up
to the branches.

← Draw textures of bark
Give a ground to your
tree

Tree branches fork like highways:

buds

EVERGREEN TREES

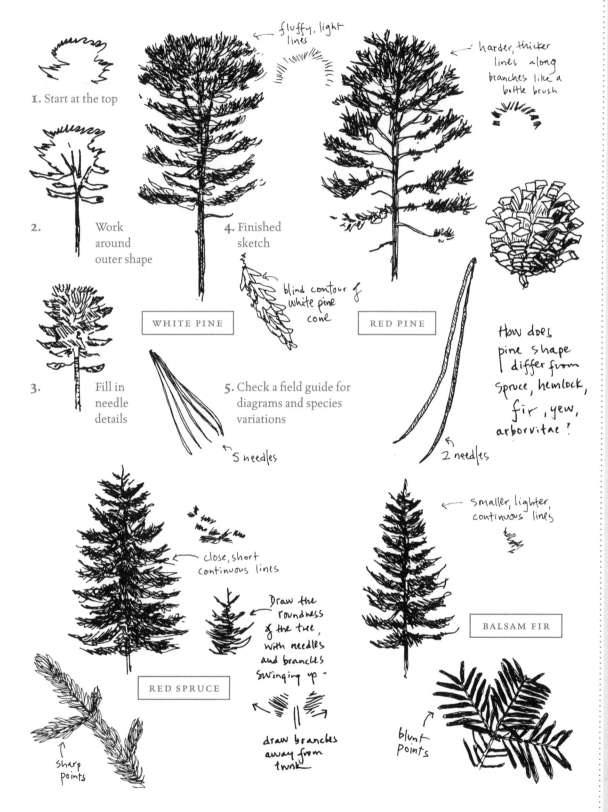

1. Start at the top

2. Work around outer shape

3. Fill in needle details

fluffy, light lines

4. Finished sketch

WHITE PINE

blind contour of white pine cone

5. Check a field guide for diagrams and species variations

5 needles

harder, thicker lines along branches like a bottle brush

RED PINE

2 needles

How does pine shape differ from spruce, hemlock, fir, yew, arborvitae !

close, short continuous lines

Draw the roundness of the tree, with needles and branches swinging up -

RED SPRUCE

draw branches away from trunk

sharp points

smaller, lighter, continuous lines

BALSAM FIR

blunt points

THINGS ON THE GROUND

Lichens, mosses, seeds, cones, fruits . . .

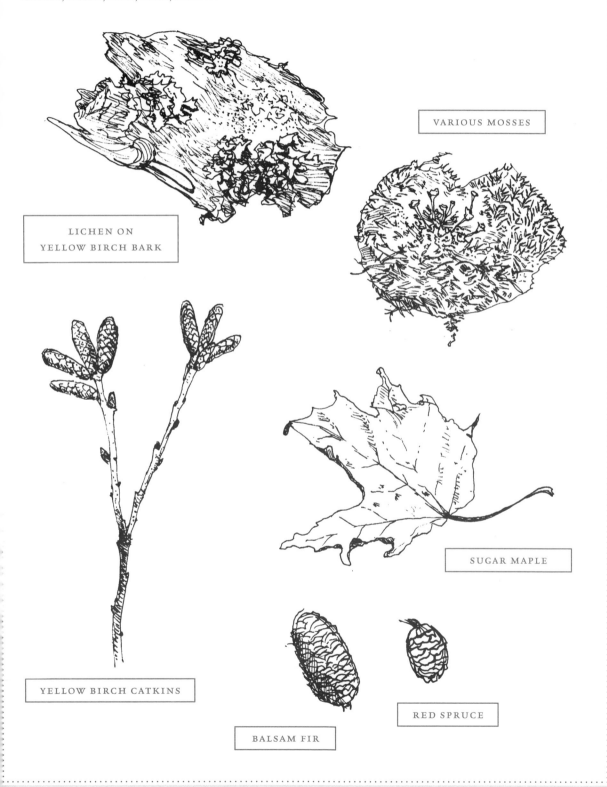

VARIOUS MOSSES

LICHEN ON
YELLOW BIRCH BARK

SUGAR MAPLE

YELLOW BIRCH CATKINS

RED SPRUCE

BALSAM FIR

SMALL ANIMALS : WILD

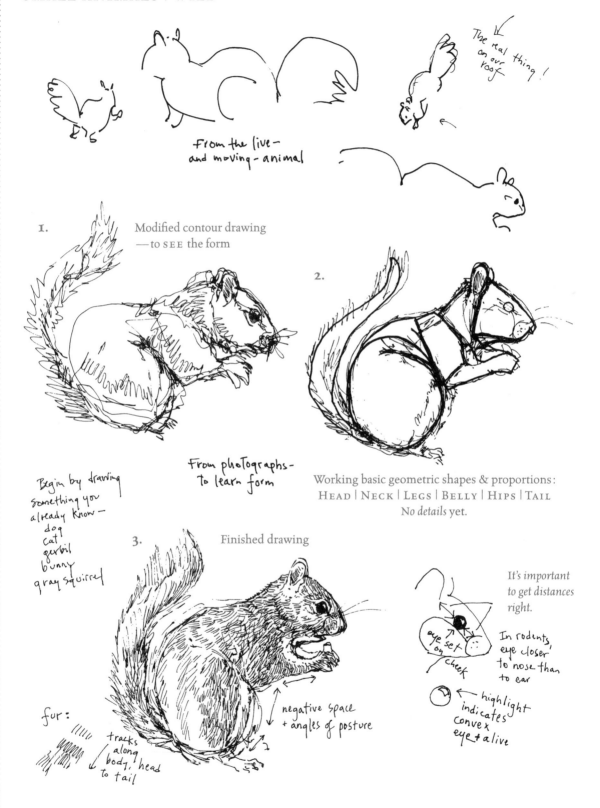

The real thing! on our roof

From the live— and moving— animal

1. Modified contour drawing —to SEE the form

2.

From photographs— to learn form

Working basic geometric shapes & proportions: HEAD | NECK | LEGS | BELLY | HIPS | TAIL No details yet.

Begin by drawing something you already know— dog cat gerbil bunny gray squirrel

3. Finished drawing

It's important to get distances right.

eye set on cheek

In rodents, eye closer to nose than to ear

highlight indicates convex eye + alive

negative space + angles of posture

fur: tracks along body, head to tail

SMALL ANIMALS : DOMESTIC

Practice drawing on your household DOG. This will help you to draw FOX, COYOTE, WOLVES.

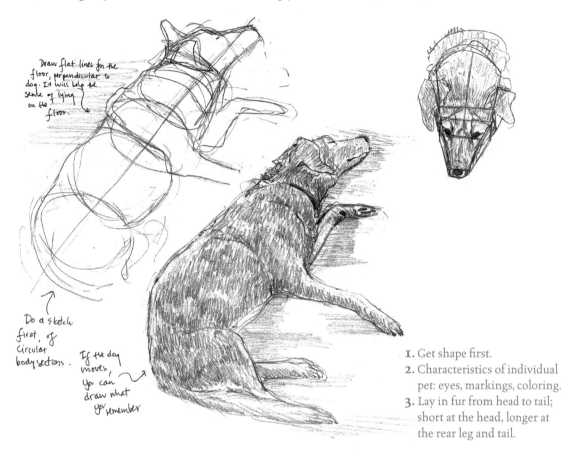

Draw flat lines for the floor, perpendicular to dog. It will help the sense of lying on the floor.

Do a sketch first, of circular body sections.

If the dog moves, you can draw what you remember

1. Get shape first.
2. Characteristics of individual pet: eyes, markings, coloring.
3. Lay in fur from head to tail; short at the head, longer at the rear leg and tail.

Practice drawing on your household CAT. This will help you to draw BOBCATS, PUMAS, JAGUARS, LIONS, and others in the feline family.

eyes can close to slits or dilate completely

profile eye

Do sketches first, getting basic shape and facial symmetry. Study the head carefully. Cats' eyes are in the front of the skull not side!

As cats move alot draw differing positions.

Much of this was sketched from memory as the kitty moved.

Cleo - 16 w.-

LARGE ANIMALS

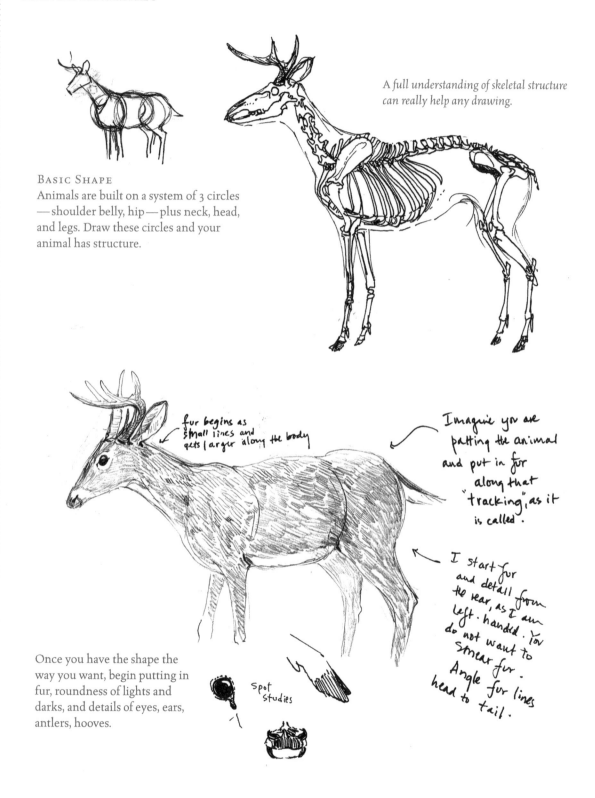

A full understanding of skeletal structure can really help any drawing.

Basic Shape
Animals are built on a system of 3 circles —shoulder belly, hip— plus neck, head, and legs. Draw these circles and your animal has structure.

fur begins as small lines and gets larger along the body

Imagine you are patting the animal and put in fur along that "tracking", as it is called.

I start fur and detail from the rear, as I am left-handed. You do not want to smear fur. Angle fur lines head to tail.

Once you have the shape the way you want, begin putting in fur, roundness of lights and darks, and details of eyes, ears, antlers, hooves.

Spot studies

PREY : Eyes on side of head

PREDATOR : Eyes in front of head

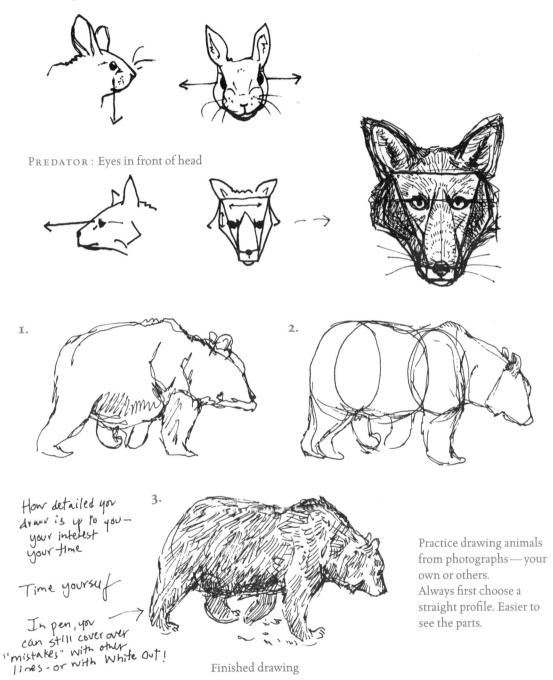

1.

2.

3.

How detailed you
draw is up to you—
your interest
your time

Time yourself

In pen, you
can still cover over
"mistakes" with other
lines - or with White Out!

Finished drawing

I knew this grizzly + had done lots of
quick drawings of her. This is from
my own photo of COCO

Practice drawing animals
from photographs — your
own or others.
Always first choose a
straight profile. Easier to
see the parts.

BIRDS

Bones are hollow so birds can fly. Greatest weight is in the chest where large flight muscles develop.

I recommend that students look closely at their next broiler chicken to find all the parts.

FEATHER GROUPINGS

The exact arrangement of the feathers will vary according to the kind of bird.

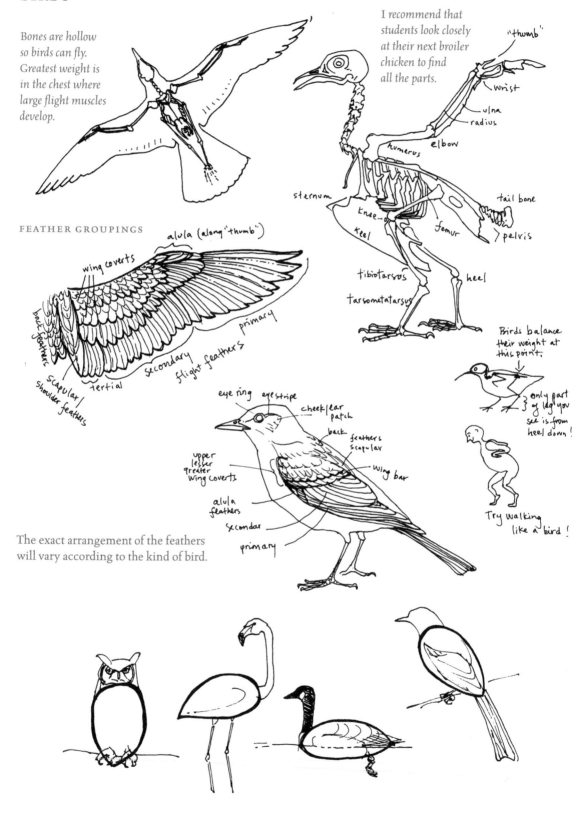

See large geometric shapes first.

From an egg, hatched...
another egg.

Draw in a sketch of the skeleton just to help position wings, tail, and feet.

WAYS TO DRAW FEATHERS:
• groups of lines within the feather groups
• draw down head and across the back
• little lines for little feathers and big lines for big feathers.

BILL:

note small eye highlight

this so bill can open!

not this

ear "patch"

EYE:

Some say the eye of an animal is the window to its soul. No highlight can indicate a dead animal (flattened eye.) Live eyes reflect light and are curved. Show highlight in upper part of eye, indicating major light source.

B.   A.

A. eye line and
B. cheek or ear patch help place eye on "face"

or natural reflective light on a convex lens

not

indicates light from a flash camera ie drawn from a photo

Feet and length of legs vary according to habitat:

Beaks vary according to use:

etc.

etc

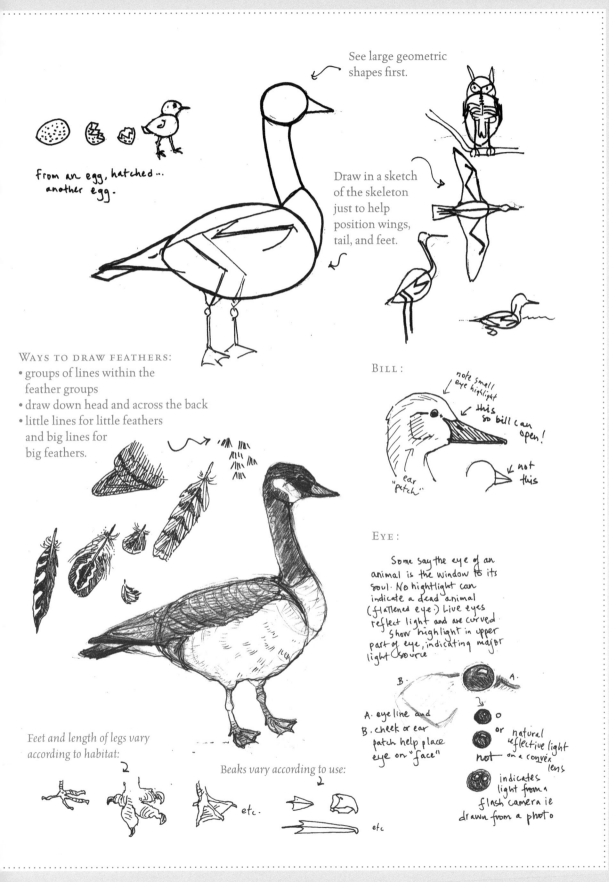

INSECTS AND SPIDERS

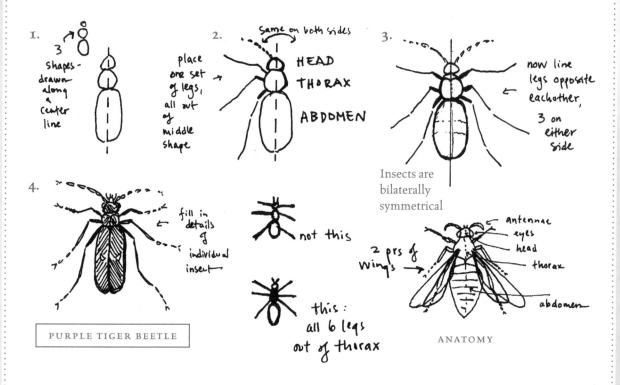

1. 3 shapes - drawn along a center line

2. place one set of legs, all out of middle shape

Same on both sides

HEAD
THORAX
ABDOMEN

3. now line legs opposite eachother, 3 on either side

Insects are bilaterally symmetrical

4. fill in details of individual insect

PURPLE TIGER BEETLE

not this

this: all 6 legs out of thorax

2 prs of wings

antennae
eyes
head
thorax
abdomen

ANATOMY

SPIDERS are related to insects, but they are NOT insects.
They each have distinctive numbers of body sections and legs

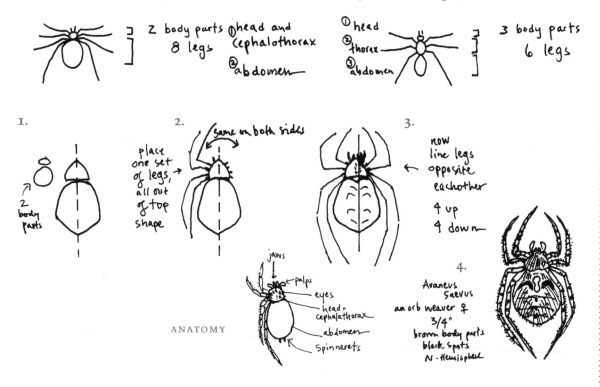

2 body parts
8 legs
① head and cephalothorax
② abdomen

① head
② thorax
③ abdomen

3 body parts
6 legs

1. 2 body parts

2. place one set of legs, all out of top shape

Same on both sides

3. now line legs opposite eachother

4 up
4 down

jaws
palps
eyes
head + cephalothorax
abdomen
spinnerets

ANATOMY

4. Araneus Saevus
an orb weaver ♀
3/4"
brown body parts
black spots
N. Hemisphere

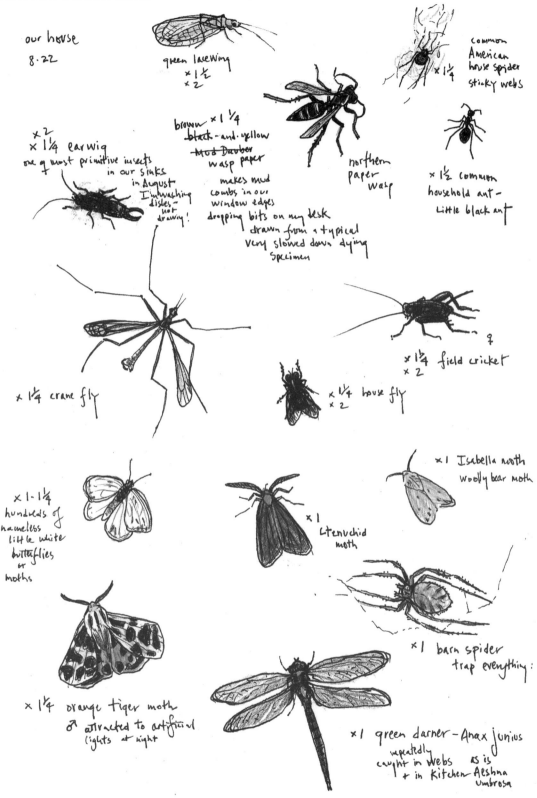

our house
8.22

green lacewing
× 1½
× 2

common
American
house spider
sticky webs
× ¼

× 2
× 1¼ earwig
one of most primitive insects
in our sinks
in August
I'm washing
dishes —
not
drawing!

brown × 1¼
black-and-yellow
Mud Dauber
wasp paper

makes mud
combs in our
window edges
dropping bits on my desk
drawn from a typical
very slowed down dying
specimen

northern
paper
wasp

× 1½ common
household ant —
Little black ant

× 1¼ crane fly

× 1¼ field cricket
× 2
♀

× 1¼ house fly
× 2

× 1 Isabella moth
woolly bear moth

× 1-1¼
hundreds of
nameless
little white
butterflies
or
moths

× 1
Ctenuchid
moth

× 1 barn spider
trap everything!

× 1¼ orange tiger moth
♂ attracted to artificial
lights at night

× 1 green darner — Anax junius
repeatedly
caught in webs   as is
+ in kitchen   Aeshna
umbrosa

REPTILES & AMPHIBIANS

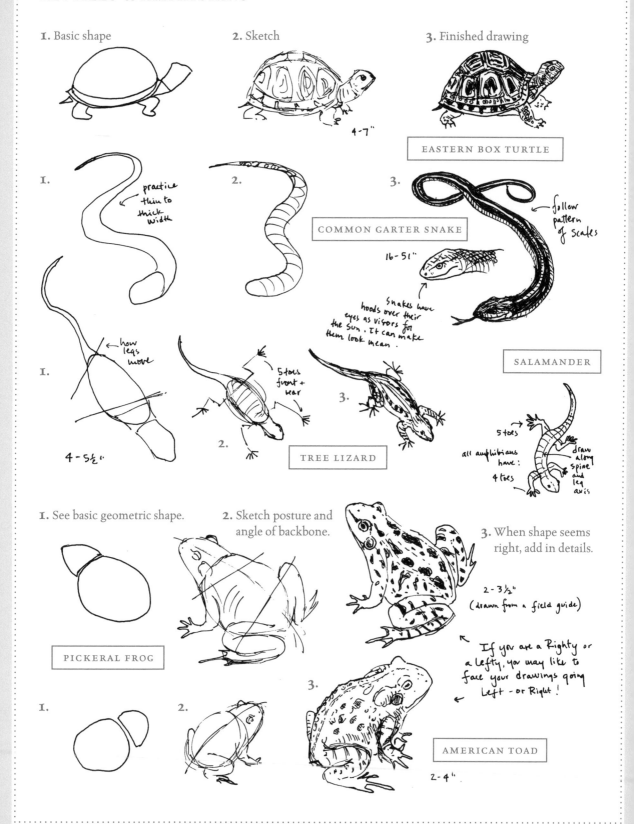

1. Basic shape

2. Sketch

3. Finished drawing

4-7"

EASTERN BOX TURTLE

1.

practice
thin to
thick
width

2.

3.

COMMON GARTER SNAKE

16-51"

follow
pattern
of scales

Snakes have
hoods over their
eyes as visors for
the sun. It can make
them look mean.

1.

how
legs
move

4-5½"

2.

5 toes
front +
rear

3.

TREE LIZARD

SALAMANDER

5 toes

all amphibians
have:

4 toes

draw
along
spine
and
leg
axis

1. See basic geometric shape.

2. Sketch posture and
angle of backbone.

3. When shape seems
right, add in details.

2-3½"
(drawn from a field guide)

If you are a Righty or
a Lefty, you may like to
face your drawings going
Left - or Right!

PICKERAL FROG

1.

2.

3.

AMERICAN TOAD

2-4"

COLLECTIONS OF OBJECTS

It's fun to collect things at different places and
times, then later draw them together indoors.

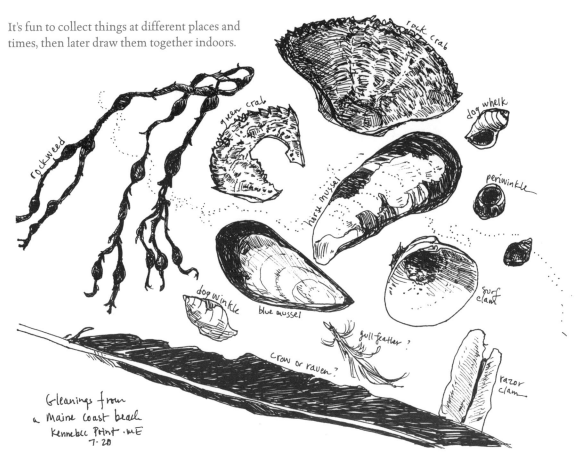

rock crab

green crab

rockweed

dog whelk

periwinkle

horse mussel

surf clam

dog winkle

blue mussel

gull feather ?

crow or raven ?

razor clam

Gleanings from
a Maine Coast beach
Kennebec Point · ME
7 · 20

TRANSITORY SUBJECTS —

Tracks, scat, snow patterns

tidy tracks
in a line
no claws
show

rear

front

SQUIRREL

sloppy
walk

CAT

6"

toe nails
show

CROW

DOG

drags
feet

front

small mammal
fur +
bones

SKUNK

rear

4 feet in a line

1½"

RACCOON

BARRED OWL
PELLET

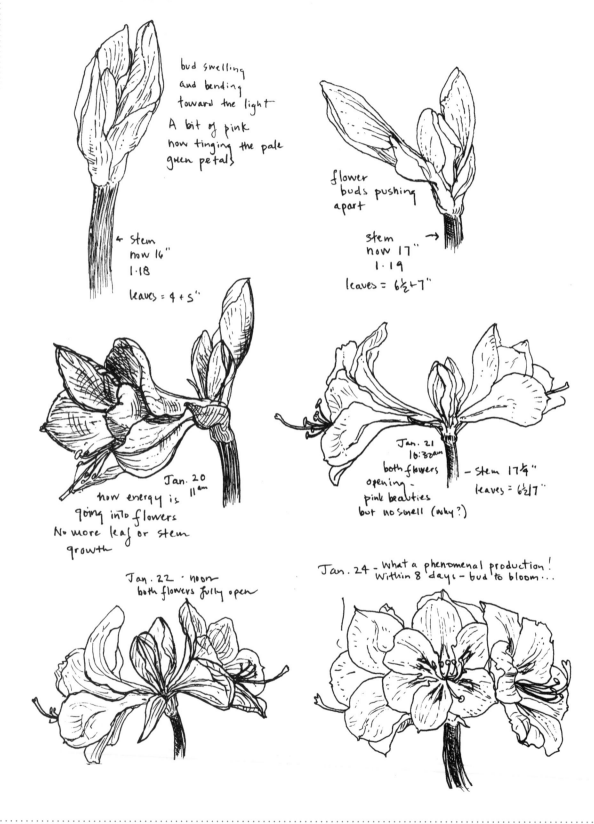

bud swelling
and bending
toward the light

A bit of pink
now tinging the pale
green petals

← stem
now 16"
1·18

leaves = 4 + 5"

flower
buds pushing
apart

stem
now 17" →
1·19

leaves = 6½ + 7"

Jan. 20
11am
how energy is
going into flowers
No more leaf or stem
growth

Jan. 21
10:30am
both flowers
opening -
pink beauties
but no smell (why?)

— stem 17¼"
leaves = 6½ |7"

Jan. 22 · noon
both flowers fully open

Jan. 24 - What a phenomenal production!
Within 8 days - bud to bloom...

OUTDOOR FLOWERS

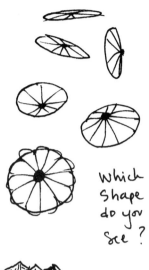

When you draw a plant with flowers, try following this sequence of steps and questions:

1. Observe the basic shape first.

2. See how the flower is put together. Where do the various flower parts — petals, stamens, pistil, leaves, stem — attach to one another? Note which parts overlap one another.

3. Keep the drawing simple. If you're doing a complex flower head, like goldenrod or ragweed, do only part of the whole.

4. Record where this flower grows; whether it is a tree, plant, or grass flower; whether it is wild or cultivated. Record the habitat in which you found it.

5. The flowers may be placed quite differently on different kinds of plants. Where is the flower on your plant placed?

6. Keep a record of when various flowers bloom over the course of a year. You can learn a lot about weather, habitat, and soil type by tracking where and when particular flowers bloom.

which Shape do you see?

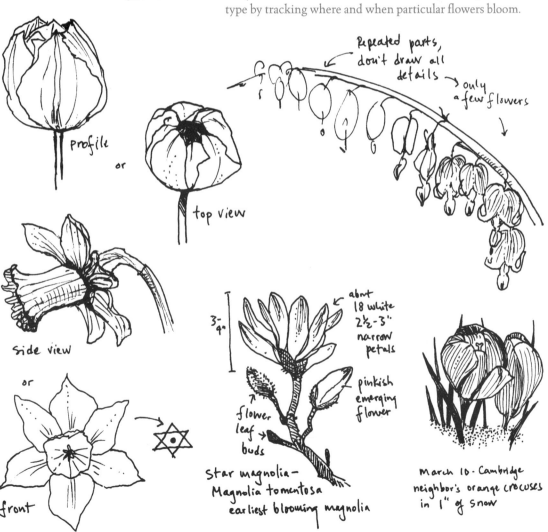

profile

or

top view

Repeated parts, don't draw all details → only a few flowers

side view

or

front

Star magnolia —
Magnolia tomentosa
earliest blooming magnolia

about 18 white 2½-3" narrow petals

pinkish emerging flower

flower leaf buds

3-4"

March 10 - Cambridge
neighbor's orange crocuses
in 1" of snow

WILDFLOWERS & WILD PLANTS

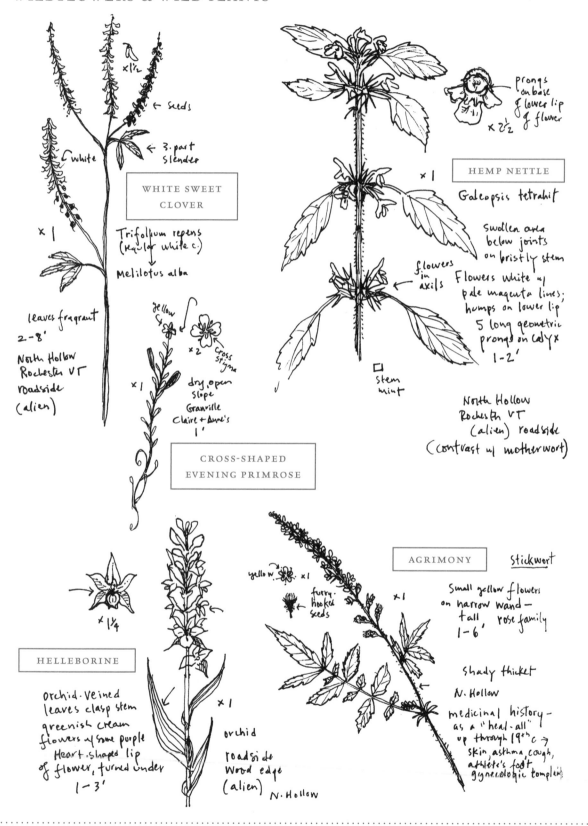

× 1½

← seeds

← 3-part
slender

white

**WHITE SWEET
CLOVER**

× 1

Trifolium repens
(regular white c.)

Melilotus alba

leaves fragrant

2-8'

North Hollow
Rochester VT
roadside
(alien)

yellow
×

× 2 Cross
stigma

× 1

dry, open
slope
Granville
Claire + Anne's
1'

**CROSS-SHAPED
EVENING PRIMROSE**

prongs
on base
of lower lip
of flower

× 2½

× 1

HEMP NETTLE

Galeopsis tetrahit

swollen area
below joints
on bristly stem

flowers
in
axils

Flowers white w/
pale magenta lines;
humps on lower lip
5 long geometric
prongs on calyx
1-2'

stem
mint

North Hollow
Rochester VT
(alien) roadside
(contrast w/ motherwort)

× 1¼

HELLEBORINE

orchid-veined
leaves clasp stem
greenish cream
flowers w/ some purple
Heart-shaped lip
of flower, turned under
1-3'

orchid
roadside
wood edge
(alien) N. Hollow

yellow. × 1

furry
hooked
seeds

× 1

AGRIMONY   Stickwort

small yellow flowers
on narrow wand —
tall, rose family
1-6'

shady thicket

N. Hollow

medicinal history —
as a "heal-all"
up through 19ᵗʰ c →
skin, asthma, cough,
athlete's foot,
gynecologic complaint

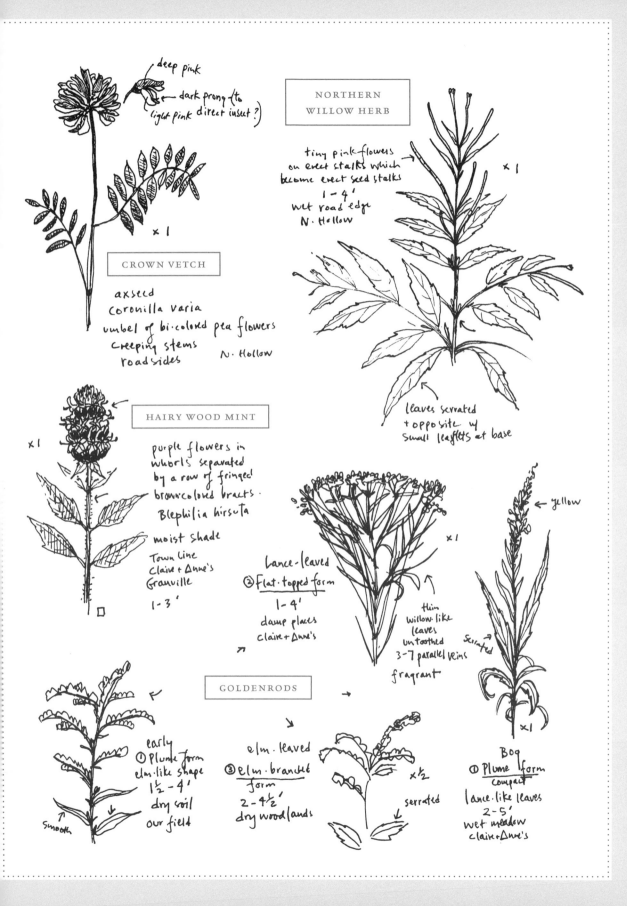

deep pink

dark prong {to
light pink direct insect?)

NORTHERN WILLOW HERB

tiny pink flowers
on erect stalks which
become erect seed stalks
1 - 4'
wet road edge
N. Hollow

×1

CROWN VETCH

axseed
Coronilla varia
umbel of bi-colored pea flowers
creeping stems
roadsides   N. Hollow

leaves serrated
+ opposite w/
small leaflets at base

HAIRY WOOD MINT

purple flowers in
whorls separated
by a row of fringed
brown-colored bracts.
Blephilia hirsuta

moist shade

Town Line
Claire + Anne's
Granville

1-3'

×1

Lance-leaved
② Flat-topped form
1 - 4'
damp places
Claire + Anne's

thin
willow-like
leaves
untoothed
3-7 parallel veins
fragrant

yellow

serrated

GOLDENRODS

early
① Plume form
elm-like shape
1½ - 4'
dry soil
our field

smooth

elm-leaved
③ elm-branched
form
2 - 4½'
dry woodlands

serrated

×½

Bog
① Plume form
compact
lance-like leaves
2 - 5'
wet meadow
claire + Anne's

×1

WEATHER

You can observe the sky, no matter where you are. I play a game with myself, when driving through particularly concrete stretches of highways or when out on open stretches of road. I watch how the cloud patterns change. The better you get at the game, the better you will get at predicting weather.

10 major CLOUD SHAPES
Have fun figuring out which is which!

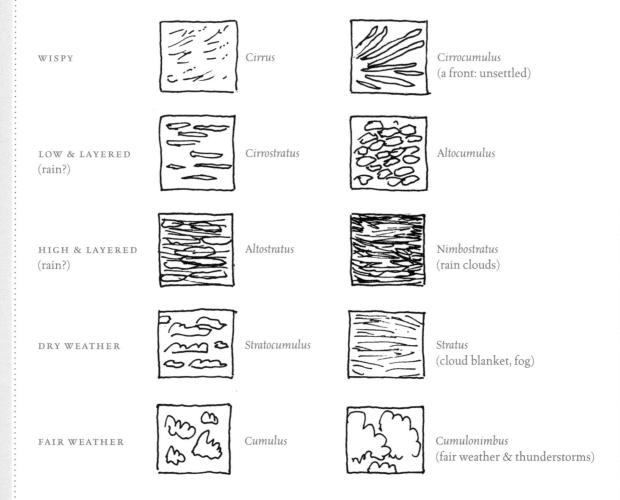

WISPY   *Cirrus*

    Cirrocumulus
(a front: unsettled)

LOW & LAYERED
(rain?)   *Cirrostratus*

    Altocumulus

HIGH & LAYERED
(rain?)   *Altostratus*

    Nimbostratus
(rain clouds)

DRY WEATHER   *Stratocumulus*

    Stratus
(cloud blanket, fog)

FAIR WEATHER   *Cumulus*

    Cumulonimbus
(fair weather & thunderstorms)

MOON PHASES:
Take in the daily shape of the moon, where it is and in what relation to the time of sunrise and sunset.

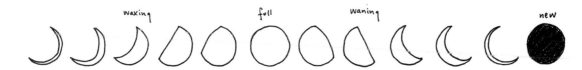

waxing   full   waning   new

Drawing the flat landscape, plus weather and river bed.

study clouds shapes and draw what you see
draw in direction of wind
horizon line is flat
flat land forms
objects for perspective
keep water lines flat
curve of river very flat

RAIN:

use watercolor
broken uneven lines at an angle; add dots where thin
puddles: lines flat + broken to show uneven surface
use colored pencil

SNOW:

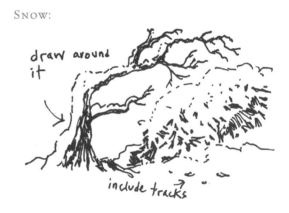

draw around it
include tracks

Where is the SUN in the sky?
Its position also determines the seasons.

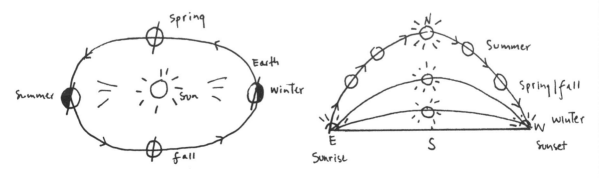

spring
Earth
winter
Sun
Summer
fall

N
Summer
spring/fall
W winter
sunset
E
Sunrise
S

LANDSCAPES

Landscapes can be very simple or very complex; 5 minutes or 65 minutes; in any medium from soft pencils to ink washes to watercolor to collage to mixed media. But, they need certain elements to work:

1. Draw a box around your landscape, to frame it like a picture. Make it no larger than 6 x 8" to begin with.

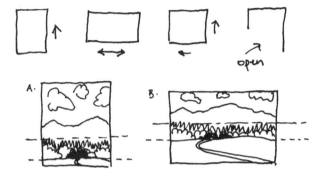

2. Landscapes tell stories. You need to help the eye of the observer travel through — from front to back, going into and out of the center.

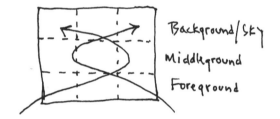

Background/Sky
Middleground
Foreground

3. Remember: objects get smaller in the distance and roads, streams, rivers seem to converge.

perspective angle

not △ or △

TRAVEL JOURNALS can be any size. I used a 2½" x 4½" when we went hiking in Idaho. I colored later in the car or motel.

Rte 84 4 pm
Oregon driving E.

EXPERIMENT with MEDIA:
This is pen, colored pencil, and watercolor.

ROCKS are like cubes, with different sides and set in three dimensions:

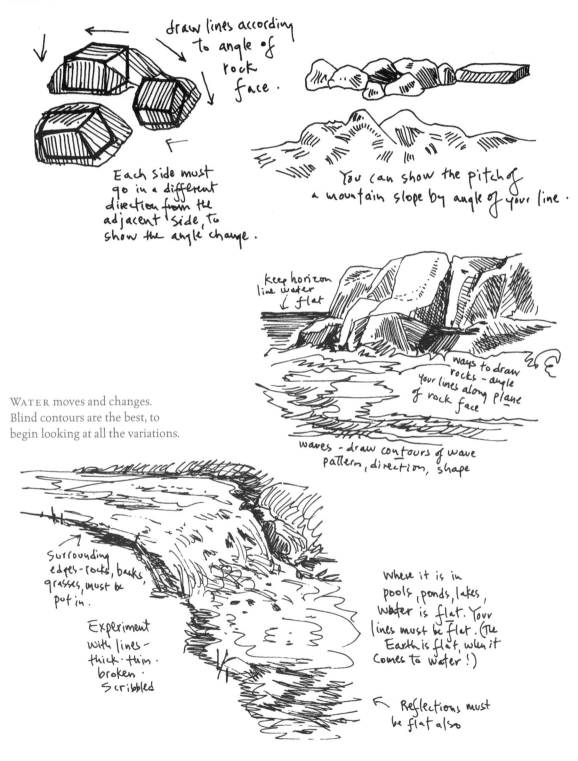

draw lines according to angle of rock face.

Each side must go in a different direction from the adjacent side, to show the angle change.

You can show the pitch of a mountain slope by angle of your line.

keep horizon line water flat

ways to draw rocks - angle your lines along plane of rock face

waves - draw contours of wave pattern, direction, shape

WATER moves and changes. Blind contours are the best, to begin looking at all the variations.

Surrounding edges - rocks, banks, grasses, must be put in.

Experiment with lines - thick · thin · broken · scribbled

Where it is in pools, ponds, lakes, water is flat. Your lines must be flat. (The Earth is flat, when it comes to water!)

Reflections must be flat also

SEASONAL SUBJECTS TO OBSERVE AND DRAW

SEASON	BIRDS	ANIMALS
AUTUMN	Observe change in activity and preparations for winter or migrations south among songbirds, hawks, geese, shorebirds. What fruits are robins, mockingbirds, and sparrows eating?	Look for signs of winter preparations, including butterfly migration, dragonfly migration, and changes in cricket, cicada, and grasshopper calls. Salamanders, slugs, spiders, sowbugs, and fish head for dark places.
WINTER	What birds stay through winter and where can you find them? Observe the habits of feeder birds: cardinals, house sparrows, mourning doves, blue jays. Look for wilder birds: owls, hawks, turkeys, ducks, vultures, crows.	What creatures stay active? What do they eat? What creatures disappear to hibernate or die? Observe animals that are active: houseflies, spiders, centipedes, rabbits, red and gray squirrels, foxes, raccoons, deer, elk, and moose. Look for tracks in the mud or snow.
SPRING	Watch for the first birds returning from the south: bay and sea ducks, warblers, sparrows. Observe activities of nearby nesting birds: starlings, house sparrows, crows, robins, cardinals.	Focus on the birth, awakening, or return of butterflies, earthworms, chipmunks, insects, frogs and toads, salmon, herring, caribou, dall sheep.
SUMMER	Learn to identify birds by their calls and habitats. Read bird guidebooks and practice drawing bird shapes: blue jay, chickadee, magpie, red-tailed hawk, song sparrow, mallard duck, herring gull, common loon.	This is the height of productivity for frogs, toads, snakes, salamanders, turtles, spiders, and earthworms. Document who is doing what. Focus on night sounds: crickets, owls, mice. Learn your local animals and draw them, learning about their habits.

PLANTS AND TREES	WEATHER, SKY, LANDSCAPES	SEASONAL CELEBRATIONS
Which plants bloom the latest: asters, goldenrod, chicory, marigolds, or butter-and-eggs? What trees and shrubs lose their leaves, turn colors? Observe and draw the varieties of tree seeds, nuts, and fruits.	Watch for weather changes. Draw cloud shapes, sunsets, rain patterns. What sounds in nature are changing? Days are noticeably shorter after September 22. Draw a little landscape scene showing tree shapes and color changes.	Autumnal equinox Sukkot Halloween Thanksgiving Day Fall festivals Year's End in Celtic calendar
Draw silhouetttes of winter trees. Observe the twig, leaf, and flower bud shapes on deciduous trees. Observe the seeds and cones of evergreens. Observe the leaves and buds of broad-leaved evergreens.	Focus on weather changes. Draw snowflake shapes. Observe rain patterns. Record moon phases. Draw constellation shapes. Days get longer after December 22. Draw a little landscape scene showing the tree and land shapes this time of year.	Winter solstice Hanukkah Advent and Christmas Kwanza Winter and New Year festivals Groundhog Day
Look for the first flowers. In the North: spring bulbs of crocus, snowdrop, daffodil. In the South: cactus, amaryllis, poinsettia. Record the first leaves and tree flowers you see. Draw sequence of flowers blooming, in high to low elevations.	Record the rain, mud, snow, and slush. Record signs of warm- and cold-weather changes. Look for animal tracks in mud. Days get noticeably longer after March 21 or 22. Draw a little landscape scene showing early signs of spring in trees and land.	Vernal equinox Internat'l Earth Day Easter Passover May Day Spring planting festivals First day of summer in Celtic calendar
Record the productivity of backyard gardens, parks, abandoned lots, fields, and meadows. Plant your own garden and draw and record its growth. Get out a field guide to plants and learn to identify what's growing where.	Use your local newspaper, radio station, TV, planetarium, and almanacs to learn about weather. Document the weather daily for a month. Days are getting shorter after June 21 or 22. Draw a little summer landscape.	Summer solstice Native American sun-dance festivals August 1 is Lammas, fall in the Celtic calender International harvest festivals

Sept. 30
monday
2:30
dark cool turns
to warm sun

[Season
[Turning

mt. A.
restlessness of
young robins
    starlings
    grackles
2 flickers
1 hooded merg-
    inser - Halcyon
stepping on acorns everywhere

hot enough
now for
cicadas

anax
in tree

angle-winged
katydid
"tick-tick-tick"

white ash
×1

Fraxinus Americana
c. 100' 200 yrs old

I recommend the following books for further study. Choose additional books according to your interests and region.

BATEMAN, ROBERT. *Thinking Like a Mountain.* Penguin Canada, 2000.

BLAKE, WENDON AND FERDINAND PETRIE. *Landscape Drawing Step by Step.* Dover Publications, 1998.

BROCKIE, KEITH. *Keith Brockie's Wildlife Sketchbook.* Macmillan Publishing, 1981.

CARSON, RACHEL. *The Sense of Wonder.* HarperCollins, 1998.

FINCH, ROBERT AND JOHN ELDER. *The Norton Book of Nature Writing.* W.W. Norton & Company, second edition, 2002.

FRANCK, FREDERICK. *The Zen of Seeing: Seeing/Drawing as Meditation.* Vintage Books, 1973.

GOLDBERG, NATALIE. *Writing Down The Bones.* Shambhala Publications, 1986.

HINCHMAN, HANNAH. *A Life in Hand.* Gibbs Smith, 1999.

JOHNSON, CATHY. *The Local Wilderness.* Prentice Hall Press, 1987.
I recommend any of Cathy Johnson's books.

LESLIE, CLARE WALKER. *Nature Drawing: A Tool for Learning.* Kendall/Hunt Publishing, 1995.

LESLIE, CLARE WALKER AND CHARLES ROTH. *Keeping a Nature Journal,* second edition. Storey Publishing, 2003.

Williams College students drawing cows in the snow
1.08 Williamstown MA

MALTZMAN, STANLEY. *Drawing Trees Step by Step*. North Light Books, 1999.

NICE, CLAUDIA. *How to Keep a Sketchbook Journal*. North Light Books, 2001.

NICOLAIDES, KIMON. *The Natural Way to Draw*. Houghton Mifflin, 1990.

STOKES, DONALD AND LILLIAN. *A Guide to Nature in Winter*. Little, Brown & Company, 1990.

WILSON, EDWARD O. *Naturalist*. Warner Books, 1995.

OTHER SOURCES

Look through the nature, science, and children's sections of bookstores and libraries. There are many illustrated field guides available; select those that are appropriate for study in your area. Nature books written between 1890 and 1950 often include beautiful illustrations. Illustrated nature journals appear and disappear rapidly in bookstores. Numbers of them come from Great Britain and Europe and are not reprinted when they run out. Check used bookstores or search Internet sites such as *www.abebooks.com* or *http://used.addall.com.*

My website is *www.clarewalkerleslie.com.*

turtle out sunning.
really seems attentive to
sounds as it swings its
head about - curious .
  facing SW morning sun
turns head to cricket
chirp -

The mission of Storey Publishing is to serve our customers

by publishing practical information that encourages personal

independence in harmony with the environment.

Storey books are available for special premium and promotional uses and for customized editions.
For further information, please call the Custom Publishing Department at 1-800-793-9396.

Book design by Kent Lew
Printed in Hong Kong by Elegance
10 9 8 7 6 5 4 3 2 1